OFF THE WALL

W9-DIV-411

A Wacky History of Germany Since 1989

A Hanel-Stern-Neuger Investigation
Inspired by Maxim Worcester

A publication of the
Frankfurter Allgemeine Zeitung GmbH Information Services
and Atlantik-Brücke e.V.

CIP-Titelaufnahme der Deutschen Bibliothek:

Off the Wall – A Wacky History of Germany Since 1989
/ Frankfurter Allgemeine Zeitung GmbH Informations-
dienste; (Hanel, Walter, [cartoons], Stern, Susan und
Neuger, James G.). – Frankfurter Allgemeine Zeitung
GmbH Informationsdienste, 1993

ISBN 3-92-9368-11-0

© 1993 Frankfurter Allgemeine Zeitung GmbH
Information Services / Atlantik-Brücke e.V.
60267 Frankfurt am Main
Typesetting: Frankfurter Allgemeine Zeitung GmbH
Information Services
Printed by: Jütte Druck GmbH, Leipzig

Printed in Germany

Contents

Foreword
(And Forewarned)

Back in the fall of 1990, after history had reputedly come to an end and started up again, an extra-special Oktoberfest was staged in the middle of Europe. On October 3, two euphoric Germanies in their early forties got hitched in a bonanza, made-for-television unification ceremony. The eyes of the planet were glued to the set as the most romantic courtship of the century came to its logical conclusion. Only when the last fireworks had fizzled and the last strains of oom-pah-pah music had died out did the international TV crews roll up their cables and leave the newlyweds to the humdrum business of everyday life.

Alas! even marriages made in heaven return, sometime or another, to terra firma. Although western Germany had sworn to love and nourish its weaker, poorer eastern mate, its enthusiasm and generosity waned by the day as it discovered just how weak and poor its mate was. And it didn't take long for eastern Germany to feel bullied, dispossessed and cheated. Squabbles broke out, scapegoats were found, and whenever tempers really flared, in rushed the TV crews. Germany-bashing, that seasonally popular sport, shot up in the ratings both at home and abroad – but especially at home, because nobody bashes the Germans better than the Germans bash themselves.

From the sidelines and from within the fray, Germany-watchers watched and wondered. What was all the fuss about? True, the cup of prosperity wasn't running over the way it had in the late 1980s (at least in the West), but it wasn't bone dry, either. To the rest of the world, united Germany was still in the pink. But the argument that they were a lot better off than most failed to cheer the Germans up – indeed, their depression (or maybe recession?) grew steadily worse.

Was the country going to the dogs or was it simply suffering from a particularly acute attack of its chronic ailment, German angst (otherwise known as worrywartitis)? Great and small minds pondered the question in academic institutions, in think tanks and on talk shows. Answers started coming in fast and furiously, but none were entirely satisfactory. Something appeared to be wrong with the way the problem was being approached, so the overall picture was distorted. Clearly, a special investigation was called for.

Enter Special Agent Hanel of the Caricature Squad and his two pen-happy sidekicks, Stern and Neuger. Throwing conventional seriousness aside, they approached the question from the humor angle. And in a few months of spadework, they came up with a very different picture. With 98 different pictures, to be precise, all commented and annotated in this riveting report. Proving that history is, most definitely, whatever you make of it.

The Off-the-Wall Folks

Boris Yeltsin

John Major

Margaret Thatcher

François Mitterand

George Bush

Mikhail Gorbachev

Helm Schn

Johannes Rau

Erich Honecker

Egon Krenz

Hans Modrow

Gregor Gysi

Manfred Stolpe

Lothar de Maizière

The Germ Mich

Hans-Jochen Vogel

Hans-Ulrich Klose

UNIT

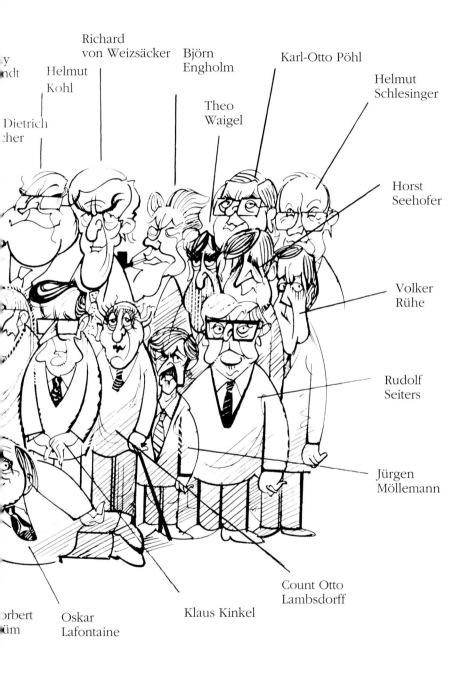

Richard
von Weizsäcker

Björn
Engholm

Karl-Otto Pöhl

Helmut
Kohl

Helmut
Schlesinger

Dietrich
cher

Theo
Waigel

Horst
Seehofer

Volker
Rühe

Rudolf
Seiters

Jürgen
Möllemann

Count Otto
Lambsdorff

orbert
üm

Oskar
Lafontaine

Klaus Kinkel

7

Meet the Off-the-Wall Folks

So you can recognize the natives rustling through these pages, here's a rundown on Who is Who, Who was Who, Who would like to be Who and Who, after the overthrow of the East German regime, was declared to have never been Who in the first place. A Who is defined as someone pictured in this book. Please note, however, that not all leading politicians are part of the story, and their omission should not be construed as an indication of non-Who status. Since in German politics, a figure can go from Who to Hooey without warning, the authors take no responsibility for the enduring validity of this list. It was, however, current as of May 1993.

Michel – Affable, dozy, unsuspecting Fritz, the centuries-old symbol of all things German. Wanders through this book as the personification of the national consciousness.

Helmut Kohl (CDU) – Chancellor of the West Germans since 1982, of all the Germans since 1990, patron saint of German unity. Thrice reelected and shooting for a fourth win in 1994.

Hans-Dietrich Genscher (FDP) – Longevity record-holder as foreign minister until his resignation after eighteen years in 1992. Prime contender for the largely ceremonial German presidency in 1994.

Richard von Weizsäcker (CDU) – Widely respected two-term holder of the aforementioned largely ceremonial German presidency.

Willy Brandt (SPD) – West German chancellor from 1969 to 1974, icebreaker in relations with the East bloc and latter-day convert to the German unity cause. Died in 1992.

Björn Engholm (SPD) – SPD party chief from 1991 to 1993, buried by the aftershocks of a bizarre provincial scandal.

Helmut Schmidt (SPD) – West German chancellor from 1974 to 1982, known for visionary pronouncements and omnipresent clouds of cigarette smoke.

Lothar de Maizière (CDU) – First and last freely elected East German prime minister, later chased from politics in Stasi scandal.

Gregor Gysi (SED/PDS) – Rebuilder of the East German socialist party (SED) into a more democratic, less flunky-ridden party (PDS) in united Germany.

Manfred Stolpe (SPD) – Highly regarded premier of eastern state of Brandenburg, dogged by allegations of collusion with Stasi under GDR regime.

Hans Modrow (SED/PDS) – Interim boss of East German government before first free elections in March 1990.

Theo Waigel (CDU) – Thickly eyebrowed finance minister and dispenser of budgetary gloom.

Count Otto Lambsdorff (FDP) – Outspoken past chief of the junior party in Kohl's center-right coalition.

Jürgen Möllemann (FDP) – Economics minister and aspirant to things higher before being derailed by influence-peddling scandal in January 1993.

Norbert Blüm (CDU) – Vertically challenged labor minister.

Oskar Lafontaine (SPD) – Head of Saarland state government, obliterated by Kohl in first post-unity election in December 1990.

Hans-Jochen Vogel (SPD) – Kohl victim in 1983 election, later SPD party chief and parliamentary whip.

Klaus Kinkel (FDP) – Filler of Genscher's foreign ministry shoes in 1992 and Lambsdorff's successor as FDP party leader.

Volker Rühe (CDU) – Defense minister since April 1992, rumored to have chancellorian pretensions.

Horst Seehofer (CSU) – Health minister, architect of draconian health-care reform (Hillary, take note).

Johannes Rau (SPD) – Popular head of North Rhine-Westphalia state government but not popular enough to unseat Kohl in 1987 election.

Hans-Ulrich Klose (SPD) – Immaculately coiffeured successor to Vogel as parliamentary whip.

Rudolf Seiters (CDU) – Holder of various government portfolios, latterly occupant of the Interior Ministry hot seat.

Karl-Otto Pöhl (SPD) – Head Bundesbank honcho and Germany's chief inflation-buster, appointed by Schmidt in 1979. Resigned in frustration in 1991.

Helmut Schlesinger (CSU) – Pöhl's successor. Steered Bundesbank through post-unity economic travails. Due to bow out in late 1993.

Erich Honecker (SED) – Wheezing, marble-mouthed commandant of the East German gerontocracy, ousted in 1989. Since then a second career as embassy squatter, fugitive from justice and Chilean tourist. Honi for short.

Egon Krenz (SED) – Honi's temporary (27-day) successor, mendacity and deceit incarnate. But otherwise a swell guy.

George Bush – U.S. president from 1989 to 1993 and chief non-German champion of unification. Later stumbled into deep domestic doo-doo.

François Mitterand – Sphinx-like French president since 1981, went from lukewarm to rah-rah in support of German unity.

Margaret Thatcher – Handbag-wielding Iron Lady, British prime minister from 1979 to 1990 and fervent supporter of NATO membership for united Germany.

John Major – Mrs. Thatcher's successor, luckless presider over Britain's harshest recession since World War II.

Mikhail Gorbachev – Otherwise foreheadly distinguished Soviet leader from 1985 to 1991. Loosened Soviet grip on eastern Europe, but later over-whelmed by forces he unleashed.

Boris Yeltsin – Populist president of post-Gorbi Russia and radical reformer.

And a few indispensable institutions:

Bundestag – Lower house of German (until 1990 West German) parliament.

Bundesrat – Upper house of parliament.

Bundesbank – Germany's central bank and guardian of the sacred D-mark.

CDU – Christian Democratic Union, Kohl's right-of-center party.

CSU – Christian Social Union, the Bavarian wing of the CDU.

SPD – Social Democratic Party, left-of-center party booted from the chancellorship in 1982.

FDP – Free Democratic Party, small center-of-center party allied with CDU/CSU in current government.

Greens – Left-of-SPD party, big on ecology, disarmament, welfare state.

Volkskammer – East Germany's rubber-stamp parliament for forty years until first free elections in March 1990. Ceased to exist on Unification Day.

SED – Socialist Unity Party, Honi's old party. By pure coincidence, regularly won 99% of the seats in the Volkskammer.

Stasi – Reviled former East German internal security – read: spook – apparatus.

And one more tip:

 is a sign used to indicate clauses in legalese.

Life Begins at Forty

*T*he year was 1989. After forty years of pumping iron in the economic fitness center, West Germans had some prodigious muscles to flex. With the most powerful economy in Europe, and the third most powerful in the world, they had manufactured, know-howed and exported their way from post-World War II rubble to global enviability. The conventional wisdom had it, however, that their biceps were unbalanced – the economic giant was a political dwarf. The western half of divided Germany had, in fact, maintained a deliberately low profile, which is just what its allies and antagonists wanted. It happily did its foreign policy workouts in the NATO gym, nurtured and watched by American, British and French coaches. It seemed like the good life could and would go on forever.

Life Ends at Forty

The year was still 1989. After forty years of oppression, suppression and economic deprivation, East Germans gave their leader, Erich Honecker, a special birthday present. They jumped out of the cake – and headed West. This came as a surprise to nobody but Honecker. With the rest of the communist world unraveling, Honi and his henchmen were the last holdouts, pitching the fiction that East Germany was a healthy industrial nation, high up in the world economic rankings. And that the Wall they had built in 1961 was to keep envious Westerners out, rather than freedom-seeking Easterners in. Snug in their luxury villas, light years removed from the common folk, they hoped the good life would go on forever. The common folk hoped otherwise.

MASS EXODUS TO D-MARKLAND!
East Germans Trek to Freedom

DITCH THE COMMIES!
Leipzig Marchers to Regime: Get Out!

Honi Regime Clings to Power

GOOD RIDDANCE!
EAST GERMANS CRACK BERLIN WALL

EUPHORIA IN WEST!
German Unification in the Cards

Hungary for Freedom

Our story begins in the summer of 1989, when many East Germans decided to vote with their feet, causing a helter-skelter exodus from Honi-land. Since a beeline over the German-German border meant certain death, prudent East German freedom seekers chose to make a slight detour via more accessible and less trigger-happy countries such as Hungary. The Hungarians, who had torn down the barbed wire separating their country from Austria in May, were supposed to send East German vacationers straight back to their worker's paradise without passing Go; still, they managed to overlook the thousands who simply walked, ran or scrambled in the western direction. Fed up with the game, on September 11, the Hungarian government told the East German government where it could get off, and the East German burghers where they could get out. Within three days, 15,000 of them had made it to West Germany, within weeks, 50,000.

That Sinking Feeling

Meanwhile, those East Germans who weren't moving out were rapidly moving in on the establishment. As summer turned to fall, the opposition entered into the party spirit, and founded in rapid succession the New Forum, Democracy Now and the Social Democratic Party. As the sea became choppier, the once-mighty Socialist Unity Party (SED) feebly tried to turn the tide by offering concessions, including safe passage to West Germany for thousands of East Germans who had holed up in the West German embassies in Prague and Warsaw and amnesty to both deserters and demonstrators. Too late. Peaceful get-togethers were all the rage, especially on Monday evenings in Leipzig, where chanting crowds of reform-hungry demonstrators swelled from a few thousand in mid-September to 300,000 by late October.

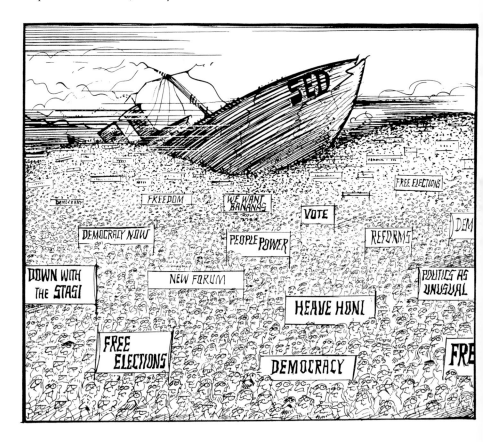

Going, Going...

With the masses thoroughly out of control, the leading party rats conspired in musty corridors to save their aging skins. Drastic action was clearly unavoidable, while real reform was unthinkable. The situation required a scapegoat. On October 18, the party elite stripped veteran state-and-party boss Honi of all his political functions – at his own request, for reasons of health – and replaced him with Egon Krenz. With buddy Honi and two other cronies sacrificed for the good of a self-chosen few, the remaining fickle fossils turned to the populace for a show of gratitude – and instead of laurels, got raspberries. As the days went by, their numbers dwindled as one after another was forced to resign.

'Cheese!'

With Honi ousted, the new man at the top, sloth-eyed, two-tongued Egon Krenz, set to work to appease and woo the people. Provided that the existing power structure remain intact, that East German socialism be kept on a steady course, and that under the motto "Change" the status quo be preserved, he was more than willing to look reality in

the eye, meet problems head-on, decide on immediate eventual measures and above all, pursue a policy of one-way dialogue. Pooh-poohing any suggestion of German unification ("There's not a soul who really wants it," he told Gorbi) and defending the Wall as a necessary bulwark between two ideologies, to show what a good guy he was, he was maybe-for-sure ready to ease restrictions on foreign travel. The wider the Krenz grin, the grimmer the public mood.

Smile, Though Your Heart Is Breaking...

With all semblance of order collapsing, on November 3, in a broadcast appeal for public confidence, Krenz announced radical reform plans and promised (honest injun) a new beginning. This failed to impress the crowd of over half a million which gathered in the nation's capital the following day. On November 5, after 21,000 people had fled the country via Czechoslovakia within 72 hours, the details of a draft law on permission to travel abroad were disclosed – only to be withdrawn as "insufficient" two days later. That same day, the cabinet resigned en bloc and the following day, the Politburo followed suit. A new Politburo to be headed by Hans Modrow was appointed by the SED Central Committee and an increasingly desperate Krenz was reduced to holding out the prospect of free and secret elections.

Off the Wall

*F*reedom to travel, or no freedom to travel? By November 9, since nobody knew what was going on any longer, that was the burning question. The Berlin Wall, that concrete symbol of repression, had for days been mobbed on both sides, as capitalist western bookmakers and the international media took bets, not on whether but on when it would be breached. And so it was that at 7 p.m., the press flack of the SED, one Schabowski by name, announced that, as an interim travel measure until a new law came into effect, East German citizens could cross into West Berlin and the Federal Republic at all border crossings. Not, of course, without an exit permit, but bureaucracy would be kept to a minimum. The last sentence fell on deaf ears; the jubilant easterners were not about to wait for a rubber stamp. The border guards, recognizing an irresistible force and fearing for their lives, let the people go.

Hey Hon, Honi, Honi, Hey Honi

Within hours on that historic November 9, over ten thousand East Berliners had joined the all-night party in West Berlin. Within days, millions of East Germans, most of them day-trippers, had poured into D-Markland – many in exhaust-spewing Trabbis, the East German answer to Mercedes. Trabbi-jams stretched endlessly. In the opposite direction, enterprising types wielding chisels rushed in to salvage bits of brick to sell on the free market (shards of Wall retailed for $14.95 plus tax in U.S. souvenir shops). Only ten months after Honi had proclaimed that the Wall would survive another hundred years, both he and it belonged to history.

Ten to One

Meanwhile, back in Bonn, the mood was euphoric, as it was throughout the country. What now? Would the opening of the border be enough to stabilize the existing East German system, or did it mark the end? What were the new game rules between the two Germanies? At the end of November, West German Chancellor Helmut Kohl, not a man to twiddle his fingers when the fate of two nations and his own place in history were at stake, jumped in with a plan with as many points as he had fingers. His idea was to gradually overcome the division of Germany via economic cooperation, then confederation and finally, federation... the specter of One Germany, albeit in a European context, took on flesh and the Allies took counsel. Bush gave his blessing; Thatcher thought and Mitterand muttered while Gorbi said, "Did I cause all of this?"

Knights on a Round Table

As things turned out, the end of the East German regime was nigh. The SED was in total disarray; after the Volkskammer (parliament) struck the supremacy of the party from the constitution on December 1, the remaining members of the old guard, including Honi-boy Krenz, threw in the towel. Now, the elevated Modrow (SED) and the appointed government (mostly SED) were as in charge as it was possible to be. As a first step to democratic reform, a Round Table was set up for discussions between representatives of the government, the various opposition groups and the church. At the first meeting on December 7, the majority came out for free elections, which were scheduled for May 6, 1990.

While professional and self-styled politicians were sitting around round tables discussing the future direction of their country, many less politically minded East Germans, still in the throes of post-Wall euphoria, were sitting in their cardboard cars discussing the direction of the nearest no-longer-forbidden city. That most German of institutions, the autobahn, became a great East-West meet market. Westophiles poured forth into the Land of Unlimited Freedom and what they saw, touched and experienced was Good.

D-Marked Men

And Good, too, was the brilliant star shining from
the hard-currency West to the funny-money East. Freedom to travel to the
pleasure palaces of capitalism was a welcome gift, but of little use to
eastern consumers as long as they could look and touch but not buy.
On the theory that the way to a people's heart is through their billfold, the
West German government handed out DM 100 in "welcome money" to
post-Wall easterners who came to check out the western merchandise.
But these limited-edition gift certificates were just an appetite-whetter.
Easterners craved more. They craved their own D-marks so they could
nonstop-shop and never drop. But how to import the legendary currency
of the West German economic miracle to the huddled, soft-monied masses
of the East? (For the answer, flip to page 37.)

The Floating of Unification

Who knows if the Germans would have thought of unifying if the rest of the world hadn't planted the idea? For months before the Wall Fall, the foreign media had gone on (and on) about the possible threat of a unified German giant with eighty million heads. Nonsense, said the wiser of those heads, it won't happen in our lifetime. But ideas once planted tend to spread, and by the end of November, the chant first heard in Leipzig in early October "We are the people" had become "We are one people." Bowing to the will of most of the populace (with free elections looming, how could they not?), the East German parties campaigned to abolish their country, and the party which promised to do so the fastest got the most votes. In the months that followed, unification took off at its own pace, while those involved in the modalities struggled to keep up...

Carpe Diem

...with canny Kohl in the forefront. Not for nothing had he read his history books and heeded the message of that great nineteenth century German unifier, Otto von Bismarck: when God goes marching through events, lad, hang on to his mantle and do the necessary. Realizing that only rapid monetary, social and political unification could prevent the entire population of East Germany from moving to the West, Kohl re-penned his ten-point plan and speeded up the timetable. With opposition spoilsports trying to deny him his destiny, he brushed aside their talk of huge costs and dire consequences and cajoled his friends on both sides of the great German divide. For he had not forgotten that elections were coming up in the traditionally socialist East. And what better way to swing East Germany's first free election than to hold out the promise of unification?

Spring 1990: Elections in East Germany

FIRST FREE VOTE

GDR Regime Fights Mushrooming Opposition

GDR Parties on the Hustings

KOHL KLONES TRIUMPH IN GDR BALLOT

Western Imports

Western Pols Woo Eastern Voters

TWO'S TOO MANY

New GDR Czar Pushes Unity Plan

Party Season

*F*ree elections call for an election campaign, and East German parties started getting their acts together. A young (41) unencumbered lawyer, Gregor Gysi, was chosen to pick up the SED pieces and give socialism a different image and the party a different name – first SED-PDS, then plain PDS. The East German Social Democrats invented themselves under Ibrahim Böhme; the East German Christian Democrats, a chip off the old SED bloc, revived themselves under the direction of musical churchman Lothar de Maizière. A new opposition party, DA, appeared on the scene. As the weeks went by, and the elections were moved forward to March 18, another new party, the conservative DSU, entered the fray, and marriages were called for. The CDU, DA and DSU forged an Alliance for Germany; the liberals formed a Union of Free Democrats, and New Forum, Democracy Now and Initiative for Peace and Human Rights became Bündnis 90. The SED and the SPD stayed single.

Alter Egos

A country with forty years (and more) of no experience with democracy, party plurality, election campaigns and politicking in general surely needs all the help it can get, and West Germany was gung-ho to give it. Each West German party chose an East German counterpart to advise, educate in western ways and go to the hustings for. As the weeks rolled by, there were those who wondered which country's parties were in the running, as Kohl and Co. battled Lafontaine and Brandt, and eastern names and faces slipped the mind. Conventional wisdom had it that the SPD would carry the day, but after forty years of communism, the people wanted more radical change. With CDU promises of speedy economic and political union ringing sweetly in their ears, 40% of the people gave Kohl's man (de Maizière) their vote. Nobody else came close.

Ave Patria

*H*aving campaigned on the One-Nation-Germany plat-
form, East Germany's new Prime Minister de Maizière could not but stick
to the score. A unity modus had to be chosen, and his fledgling coalition
opted to become part of the Federal Republic by simple accession; the five
historical East German states, dissolved by the communists, would recon-
stitute themselves and join the West German eleven. The date of the wedding was left open, and de Maizière was all for playing it molto adagio.
Cold feet? Perhaps. As the terms of the marriage contract were negotiated,
he realized sadly that this was less a union than a takeover and that his
country was in danger of being smothered. To get favorable conditions,
he'd have to put on the performance of his life.

Friends Indeed

Allies Back Unity Gambit

IN OR OUT?

SOVIETS ON NATO ROLE: NYET!

The New Math

Two Plus Four Equals One

GORBASM!

SOVIET BOSS OKAYS NATO MEMBERSHIP

WORLD WARMS TO UNITY IDEA

Pillars of Support

After the initial discombobulation at the prospect of a single Germany, the Allies rallied royally. Thatcher and Mitterand reassessed where their interests lay and, without too much ado, joined the more enthusiastic Bush in signaling shades of green to speedy unity. Gorbi, whose perestroika had led to the situation in the first place, could hardly halt the inexorable tide. So Gorbi, so the rest of the Warsaw Pact countries, and soon, friends and ex-foes were all at one with oneness. At least in principle. There remained, however, weighty matters to be settled, as the realization sunk in during the heady spring that the old world order had truly gone forever and a new one would have to be found. Who would be friends with whom in the international alliance game, and at whose table (if any) would the new Germany sit?

My Heart Belongs to NATO

The question of military alliances had come up early in the negotiating game. Obviously, one country could hardly belong to two antagonistic camps, which despite détente, still had a tenuous relationship. Modrow, backed by Gorbi, first stumped for a neutral united Germany, a solution Kohl rejected out of hand. He wanted all of Germany in NATO, which, not surprisingly, was what NATO wanted too. By the time the foreign ministers of the Warsaw Pact countries met in March, most were quite sanguine about the prospect of Germany in NATO, and only the Soviets formally objected. How resigned they were to the inevitable is not clear, but during Kohl's July visit to Gorbi in the Caucasus, the two leaders got cracking, and Kohl returned triumphantly with Germany tucked in NATO's pocket.

Two Plus Four Equals One

During the spring and summer of 1990, plans to recreate Germany were proposed, rejected and amended at breakneck speed, as telephone lines buzzed and decision-makers hurtled from one meeting to another. To oversee those aspects of unification which were of primary concern to the non-Teutonic world, a series of conferences, dubbed the Two-Plus-Four Talks, were held between May and September. The four were the foreign ministers of the victorious World War II powers, the two, the Germanies they had created, and the agreement they came up with was in lieu of a never-finally-negotiated end-of-war peace settlement. Germany agreed to recognize its existing borders, renounce territorial claims for ever and ever, amen (see page 43), and reduce its (combined) military force, which might only fire a shot in self-defense. In return, the victors returned to Germany its full sovereignty.

CASH & CARRY
East to Get D-Mark on Juicy Terms

SPD Balks at Money Deal

D-DAY!
D-MARK GOES EAST

Consuming Passions
Easterners in Shopping Frenzy

Slumping Economy Sours Eastern Mood

Balance Due

*N*early 300,000 East Germans packed up their troubles and skipped off to West Germany between the de-Walling on November 9, 1989 and the elections on March 18, 1990. Unless the "influx" were "stemmed," opined the pundits, easterners would depopulate their country and unify Germany on western soil. And the best influx-stemmer was the D-mark itself. On March 20, all of East Germany marked Helmut Kohl's words. The two German economies would merge, he said, bringing a currency that was actually worth something to the downtrodden East. Negotiations would determine the how, the when and the currency conversion modalities. On the free market, it took seven lowly East-marks to buy one princely D-mark. But a seven-for-one exchange rate would give East Germans as little buying power as before. So the West German government agreed on a one-to-one swap for cash, salaries, rents and pensions. Could the money deal balance the two starkly mismatched economies?

No Way

"**N**o, no, no! It's a raw deal!" shouted frantic Oskar Lafontaine, and accused the government of monetary maxi-madness. But neither the SPD chancellor candidate nor the chieftain of the mighty Bundesbank (see page 70) could deter the power-wielders from sealing their one-to-one promise in an economic, monetary and social treaty that would essentially mate the two countries before the formal wedding ceremony. Oskar watched with horror as the treaty was celebrated on May 18 and, in a last attempt to avert what he saw as arithmetic catastrophe, persuaded a majority of his party to refuse to ratify it. To no avail. The treaty was approved by both the Bundestag and the Volkskammer on June 21, to take effect ten days later.

Secrets of the Temple

      And so it was that the D-mark finally came to town on July 1. At midnight East Germans rushed to their friendly neighborhood temple (the nearest branch of a West German commercial bank) and found it full of late-working tellers. Wild scenes of jubilation ensued, as if the Savior Himself were making a deposit or withdrawal. The East Germans made both. Plunking down their now-worthless East-marks, they were handed a wad of West German legal tender and commanded: Go forth and multiply your wealth in the divine state of grace that is the free market. But like the sacred Ten, the profane Eleventh Commandment proved maddeningly difficult to fulfill. Upon exiting the temple, the eastern capitalists-in-waiting stumbled across one worry after another on the road to the promised land.

Something's Fishy

D-marks in hand, the man from the East crawled out of his socialist clothes and went for a skinny-dip in the fountain of economic youth. It was a chilling experience for the stunted shopper whose expectations had been inflated by TV commercial jingles promising umpteen brands of gourmet dog food for the discerning canine and sensor-activated dental plaque removers. No, easterners did not always get on swimmingly in the open market. In the pool were sharks – loan and otherwise – with an icy determination to separate them from their freshly minted western cash. Dubious financial advisers roamed the eastern lands, guaranteeing to double or triple their wealth, pain-free and virtually overnight. But when our eastern friend woke up the next day, his money and the financial sharpie were long gone – and with them his unbounded faith in the free market.

Little Market Economy of Horrors

From the start, East Germany was capitalistically challenged. Its overstaffed, miserably equipped, debt-infested companies were woefully inefficient at producing shoddy products that virtually no one wanted anyway. Not least the East Germans themselves. Have D-mark, will splurge on hitherto untouchable West German goodies, was the general mood. Nor were fraternal ties to former socialist brethren of much help. The breakdown of trading relationships in the broken-down Soviet bloc put the final kibosh on East German industry. Most companies had been owned and mismanaged by the socialist state, so it was no wonder that running one was all cost and little benefit. But as free-enterprise ghouls spooked eastern industry into submission, Kohl promised to carry it to a new castle.

GERMANY, POLAND BURY BORDER HATCHET

COLLAPSE!
Eastern Economy on the Rocks

East Staggers into German-German Marriage

Oh Happy Day!
Unification Set for October 3

TOGETHER AGAIN!
GERMANY UNITES AFTER 45 YEARS

The Dragged Foot

*T*he non-issue of the season was the form and forum in which the united Germany would recognize its border with Poland. Only those Germans in their rightist of minds held out hopes of winning back parts of western Poland which had been under German control prior to Hitler's war. The irredentists were a tiny lobby, but a noisy, irritating and

politically potent one. In reaffirming Germany's commitment to existing international borders, the chancellor spoke too softly and carried too small a stick for his domestic detractors and foreign benefactors. France in particular ran true to its old form of getting chummy with Poland whenever Germany gets uppity. The storm finally blew over in June, when a Bundestag resolution upheld the inviolability of the border and promised to settle the issue in a bilateral treaty.

For Whom the Suit Fits

Once the side-effects of currency union had made them-selves felt, the already tottering economy took a further nosedive. Fearful and confused, the East German nation, no longer sure what was causing its ills, heaved with unrest. A shotgun wedding became inevitable, as de Maizière struggled to preserve both his and the country's sanity, and Kohl & Friends pointed to the end of the rainbow. In August, the nuptials were set for October 3 and wise and other-wise men worked feverishly to finalize a viable unity treaty. It was a one-way affair. With West Germany promising to take over all East German debts and responsibilities, to harmonize and privatize everything in sight, to mandate, delegate, regulate and stipulate, East Germany could only let it happen.

Birthday Baby

And happen it did. On October 3, 1990, Germany lost a country but gained five new states, 108,813 square kilometers, seventeen million people and a load of problems and blessings, big and small respectively. Europe lost some of its equilibrium through its weightier partner, but stood to gain another Euro-talk language on a par with English and French. The world lost and gained it knew not what, but figured that time would tell it. As proud daddy Kohl paraded his baby on that Day of Days, the folks at home and abroad paid their respects and wished the newborn well. But did all the bells ring out, or did some toll?

**Undivided Joy
at the
Brandenburg Gate,
Berlin,
October 3, 1990**

CDU CLEANS UP IN EASTERN STATE VOTE

Parties Swap Blows in Grueling Campaign

Comeback Kid?
Underdog Oskar Soldiers On

KING KOHL!
HELMUT HAMMERS OSKAR

GENSCHMAN THE GREAT!
FDP Boosts Coalition Influence

Einheit = Unity

Partisan Warfare

    After the fireworks and sparklers of October 3, the parties trotted out heavier artillery with live political ammunition for the freshly united country's first election season. On October 14, eastern German voters picked state-level parliaments. Flush from the unity bash, they handed broad pluralities to unifier Kohl's Christian Democratic party in every eastern state but one. That set the stage for the December 2 Bundestag vote, the first free and secret all-German election since 1932. Would the unity chancellor win a ringing endorsement from a grateful populace? Or, shades of Churchill, would he be bounced out of Bonn at the moment of triumph? Taking no chances, Kohl ran a bomb-proof campaign.

Fitful Oskar

With the chancellor basking in unity glory and the still-blooming economy, opponent Lafontaine sweated through the Herculean task of mounting a halfway credible challenge. "Yes, but" had been his party's standard line on Kohl's all-out ten-month dash to unification. While Kohl promised a unified German rose garden, at least in the intermediate term, the Social Democrats fretted about paying the gardeners. Voters could read Oskar's lips: Yes, new taxes. The incumbent meanwhile asked: Are you better off now than you were one year ago? Helmut smiled while Oskar slogged. As usual, it was politics.

Here's the Beef

On December 2 the people voted early and late, and they voted often for Kohl and Genscher in a landslide victory for more of the same. The CDU picked up 44%, the FDP – the country's classic swing party – a muscular 11% of the vote. Lafontaine led the SPD to its worst electoral drubbing since 1957, with 33.5%. The balance went to Greenies, socialist retreads and splinter parties. "King Kohl & Big Genschman," trumpeted Germany's biggest-circulation tabloid. Old King Kohl beamed, with a bit of poetic license, over the "best election results ever achieved by a democratic party in Germany." Brawny Genschman went into the coalition negotiations stronger than ever, raising the bushily mistrustful eyebrows of Theo Waigel, chief of the CDU's Bavarian sister party.

Autumn 1990 to Autumn 1991: Post-Unity Worries

Paymasters
Germans Bankroll Anti-Saddam Coalition

YUCK!
Taxes Soar to Pay for Unity

Eastern Economy Bludgeoned
by Socialist Legacy

Bonn Voyage!
BUNDESTAG TO MOVE TO BERLIN

PSYCHED OUT
Worries Cloud United Germany's First Birthday

Cloud Cuckoo Land

German foreign policy could run, but it couldn't hide from the global burdens thrust upon it by unification and the end of the East-West standoff. Comfortably ensconced in the Atlantic Alliance for forty years, West Germany had let its bigger NATO brothers (mainly the Yanks and Brits) call (and fire) the shots. Its constitution forbade troop deployments except in alliance self-defense. Uncomfortably jammed into the Warsaw Pact (Warpak™) for the same forty years, East Germany had surrendered all foreign policy autonomy to the friendly tovariches in the Kremlin. The new Germany would have to come out of the clouds. But however gingerly it stepped toward earth, it incurred the wrath of critics. Some feared it would be too strong; others, too weak.

It Walks, It Talks, It Says NATO

*T*o quell foreign fears of a new German juggernaut, Genscher took the roly-poly unity baby on roadshows in world capitals and at the United Nations. In November 1990, members of the cold-war-ring factions met to bury the hatchet at a Paris parley of the Conference on Security and Cooperation in Europe. Playful Mr. Unity charmed away world worries that the Big D (= Deutschland) would throw its weight around in the shakily reunited Europe. Germany wouldn't go on any non-NATO adventures, he promised. Nor would it covet a seat on the UN Security Council. It joined 32 western and eastern European states plus the United States and Canada in affirming "democracy as the sole form of government." All well and good – but conflicts in the world's hotter spots would soon test Germany's and Europe's resolve.

Breakfast Crunch

Agog with unity glee, the Germans paid comparatively little attention to the ghastly happenings on the industrialized world's southern flank. On August 2, as the Two-Plus-Four Talks were nearing their conclusion, Iraqi strongman Saddam Hussein dispatched his armies to reclaim his country's nineteenth province (his view) or maul innocent, oil-producing Kuwait (the civilized world's view). Throughout the fall, U.S. troops arrived in neighboring Saudi Arabia to prevent further Saddamy and, eventually, bomb the infidels back into stone-age Iraq. While America spent its peace dividend in the Middle Eastern sands, Germany woke up to the beastly reality that national security wasn't just for breakfast anymore. From now on, it was a full-time job.

Fiscal Education

But enough about foreign entanglements: back to the domestic hoopla. During the fall 1990 election campaign, the escalating costs of repairing the economically demolished East had been a wide-open secret. So much so that the unity chancellor saw little reason to dwell on the inevitability of higher taxes and other unpleasantries. Thus no one should have been surprised when, in 1991, the government conjured up a variety of party-pooping fiscal measures. It imposed a 7.5% "solidarity sur-tax," raised the already draconian gas tax, hiked the insurance premium tax and puffed up the tobacco tax. And in an astonishing feat of fiscal acrobatics, it managed to go far deeper into the red than it had ever been before.

Desocialized Medicine

Before departing the scene, the socialist government in March 1990 had deposited all the companies it owned – in other words, the whole of East German industry – into the world's biggest commercial holding pen: the Treuhandanstalt. Which is to say: Troyhont. Founded by socialists to hasten the state's retreat from economic life, the Treuhand was turned by capitalists into the mother of all bureaucracies. Its mission: find western buyers for the viable companies, give the nonviable ones a proper burial – and commiserate with the employees left jobless in the process. The job of bankruptcy trustee for over 12,000 companies was a thankless one. The Treuhand was permanently in the crossfire. One day that fire was all too real. The agency's first western German director, business executive Detlev Rohwedder, was shot to death by terrorists on April 1, 1991.

Homebody

Private property is what makes capitalism fun and socialism a drag – but who knew who owned what in the eastern states? Before World War II, a man's home was his castle, and the man had a deed to prove it. Then the communists (of Russian and East German stripe) showed up, seized private and corporate property and farmland and started barking orders. When the bark subsided to a whimper in 1990, the communist government still had title to everything in sight. From Dresden to Düsseldorf to Detroit, onetime owners of eastern German property clamored to get their possessions back. Only the shadowy land registers knew whether an old owner's claim was legit or not. The records that hadn't been lost or destroyed were in grubby shape after four decades in cobweb-filled basements. The courts would take decades to sort it all out. The lawyers would rejoice for an equal period of time.

Ward of the State

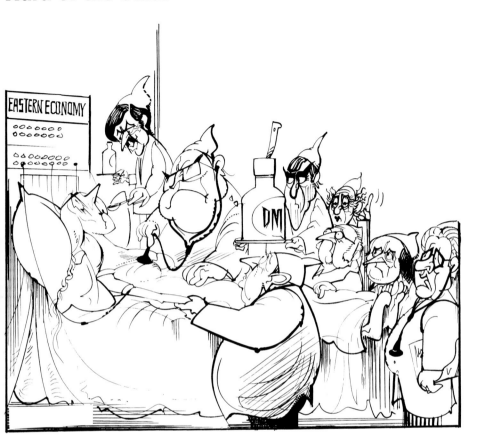

After wheezing and coughing through the unification process, the heavily sedated eastern economy came down with a near-terminal case of high inflation pressure and unsightly unemployment rashes. Paramedics stabilized the spluttering, delirious patient and rushed her to the Bonn Institute of Internal Commercial Medicine. A tripartisan team of seasoned health-care professionals discovered there was nothing ailing the patient that a massive intravenous transfer of D-marks could not cure. And so the specialists prescribed a monetary infusion in an uncommonly high dosage to patch up her battered infrastructure, revive her unproductive companies and retrain her people for the capitalist workplace. At over a hundred billion marks yearly, the bill for the experimental drugs further strained the West's embattled health-care system.

Vultures, Vultures Everywhere

Determined to tighten its belt and pinch its pfennigs, the government did its best to scare off the spending vultures. But they would not be denied. Eastern Germany and eastern Europe had ravenous appetites. In the Persian Gulf, the unholy dictator refused to give back the petroleum principality of Kuwait. Booting him out would be expensive and explosive. The constitution forbade German troops from directly taking part in the operation that drove the invaders back inside the Iraqi border. But in good NATO-ly solidarity, there was something Germany could contribute: money. So as it talked the austerity talk, the government walked the war-financing walk. When officials of the Kuwait-salvation army came calling, the charitably minded Germans promptly made out a DM 11 billion check. That sent one vulture flapping back whence it came. But the others continued to roost.

Keg Party

Remember the Soviet Union, a.k.a. Evil Empire? By 1991 the once-feared superpower was a superpauper. Perestroika and glasnost, the twin pillars of the Gorbonic method, had destroyed the country in order to save it. Political chaos threatened. Long-suppressed ethnic rivalries seethed in the economic wreckage. Staring at the mess, the Soviet Union's conquerors avoided high-fives and We're Number One gestures. Their former enemy had them over a barrel. Cleaning up the debris would require loads of money. Their money. Preferably German money – the best money money could buy. So to work off their unification debt to Gorbachev, the Germans paid off some of his.

Punished Capital

Before the new and improved Germany's government could have business cards printed up, it had to decide on a domicile. It was a moot point to those who felt drowsy Bonn had served West Germany just fine for four decades. A debatable point, said strict constructionists of the West German constitution of 1949, which enshrined Berlin's capital legitimacy and made Bonn a temporary deputy. Bonn had forty years of liberal democracy and western European integration going for it. Berlin had its historic, if somewhat tarnished, role as the center of all things German. Plus it had sixteen million eastern Germans with a hankering for a capital in their own backyard. In the June 1991 Bundestag vote, eastern representatives tipped the balance in Berlin's favor, 338 to 320. But Bonn stayed alive and unburied – and will probably remain so into the next century.

And Many Happier Returns

      On United Germany's first birthday, it was in the throes of growing pains and showing signs of exhaustion. Gone was the euphoria of the year before. The bells had indeed tolled for many eastern Germans who were grappling with massive unemployment, galloping inflation, their police-state legacy (see next section) and constant, hitherto unknown fears about the future. Kohl's promise that unification would do no harm to nobody had not been kept and bitterness was in the air. And the western Germans were griping too; they had not been prepared for the staggering costs of unification and brotherly love was being sorely stretched. Birthday speakers throughout the land cautioned against pessimism and talked of good days to come...sometime.

Torrent of Stasi Exposés
WERE WE ALL SPIED ON?

Ex-Spooks Dash for Cover

The Heads Are Rolling
STASI WARLORDS UNMASKED

OPEN SECRETS
Spook Files Unlocked for Public Access

STOLPE FIGHTS STASI REVELATIONS

Next Please

Most monsters cease to be malignant after they die, but the evil of the Ministry of State Security (known as Stasi, and not just to its friends) lives on. The self-dubbed "sword and shield of the Party" continues to terrorize, but is turning on new victims – its own former eyes and ears. For three decades the creature of Erich Mielke and his 100,000 full-time spooks, Stasi had a bottomless bag of dirty tricks to enlist its countless freelance spies and informers and infiltrate every level of society. As revelations of cooperation with the Stasi caused heads to roll, one public figure after another disappeared from the scene. The people cheered, but not for long. Soon other heads were exposed – those of neighbors, friends and family.

Stasi, Stasi Everywhere

The Gauck commission, set up in October 1990 to assemble and administer those Stasi files which had not been deliberately destroyed during the Modrow months, could calculate its work in distance. In over 120 remaining miles of documents, twelve miles were comprehensive dossiers on individuals – about six million of them, a third of the population. Outraged and frightened, citizens demanded the right to know if they had been among the chosen many, and if so, insisted on access to their files. In January 1992, the files were made available to their victims. The first to read their lives returned with horror stories of betrayal and manipulation. With millions still queuing up for the moment of truth, the show goes on...and on.

A Thorough Facial

*T*he Stasi blackmailed, arm-twisted and induced around 150,000 informants to rat on their fellows. But when is to inform not to inform? Many of those accused of collaboration protest their innocence; they claim that any contact with the Stasi was unwitting, harmless or absolutely necessary in the pursuit of a better life for themselves and others. Manfred Stolpe, erstwhile lay head of the Protestant Church in the East, was a recognized and respected go-between in the complicated, delicate relationship between church and state. A hero to the dissidents he helped, the man who is now the popular Social Democratic leader of the state of Brandenburg has been waging a seemingly endless battle to clear his name.

UP, UP AND AWAY
Inflation on the Loose

Seeya!
Bundesbank Boss Hits Ejection Button

MAASTRICHT DEAL TO FORM EUROMONEY UNION

National Treasure in Peril
SAVE THE D-MARK, GERMANS CRY

Soaring Rents Hurt House-Hunters

Fall from Grace

*T*here is a season for all things. A time to be born, a time to die – even a time for the world's stoutest currency to buckle under the incalculable burdens of German unification. That time came toward the end of 1991. The post-unity boom was spent, and now the people would be taxed. And the government would go on a borrowing binge. Suddenly, the specter of inflation was abroad in the land. Germany's currency for all seasons lost 3.5% of its buying power in 1991, 4% in 1992. Hardly the killer inflation of 1923, when restaurant prices went up while customers were eating, printers gave up trying to print numbers on bills, and a single dollar ended up buying 4,420,000,000,000 marks. Since that monetary nightmare, Germans have writhed in agony at the slightest inflationary twitch. But not to worry, said the politicians: The D-mark will surely bloom again.

Pöhl's Apart

But it would no longer bloom under Karl Otto Pöhl, the outspoken Bundesbank chief who had stepped down in April 1991 after a long-running feud with the Bonn policy people. Germany's grand central banker had been less than enthusiastic about the generous exchange rate the Kohl government offered East Germans in the July 1990 economic merger. Back then, Pöhl had predicted that the immediate introduction of the D-mark on a one-to-one basis could push the hyperventilating eastern economy over the edge. Jobs would crumble as noncompetitive state-run dinosaur-companies were priced out of the world market. Which is what, ahem, happened. But the fulfillment of the direst prediction is no consolation to the predictor. Worn out by politicking and fearful that the economic worst was yet to come, Pöhl made way for fresh (if somewhat older) blood...

Bundesbank Irae

...in the priestly person of Helmut Schlesinger, an academic economist and longtime Bundesbank insider with the halo of monetary invincibility. Physically and personality-wise, the new man in the central banking hot seat was a study in contrasts to the bouncy and flamboyant Pöhl. Policy-wise, Schlesinger was an even more devout believer in Germany's secular religion: tight, inflation-proof money. To whip inflation before inflation whipped Germany, he continued Pöhl's policy of ratcheting up interest rates to smother money-supply expansion. That checked inflation alright. But it also deepened the recession Germany was stumbling into – and, some neighbors alleged, spread the economic misery across Europe.

For a Good Time, Call...

To escape doldrums at home, in December 1991 the matronly D-mark and her escort, Michel, went on a weekend getaway to the Dutch city of Maastricht. Rumor had it that the heads of the twelve European Community governments were also in town. Maastricht was full of seductive and illicit (and potentially expensive) pleasures. Michel looked longingly at ECU, the possible future pan-European currency. Would he leave the comfortable embrace of D-mark for the shapely but mysterious ECU? Economists urged him to do it. Nothing against his long-time squeeze, they said, but she was far too domestic and didn't travel well. ECU would show him a good time all across Europe. Deep down, Michel knew they were right. But could he get up the courage to spurn his childhood sweetheart? In Maastricht, everything was up for grabs.

Inhuman Sacrifice?

*F*rom a sacred place in Maastricht, a peculiar rite
flickered across TV screens back in Germany. The high priest of German
unification was carrying a terrified lamb to its sacrificial death in the flames
of European monetary integration. Anglican and French holy men vowed
to make similarly burnt offerings. The devout German audience did not
know whether to respond with shock or reverence. Had their harsh and
forbidding god really willed such an act? The nation breathed a palpable
sigh of relief when word came that the mirages from Maastricht were only
a dress rehearsal. The actual sacrifice would not take place until 1997.
Or was it 1999? The European money god had sent confusing messages.
But some German disbelievers, concentrated in the state of Bavaria,
weren't taking any chances. They plotted to spirit the lamb to safety when
its tormentors returned.

You Dirty Rat

Fast cars aren't all that Germany exports. News that German ingredients had found their way into Iraqi chemical weapons and SCUD missiles seriously blotched the reputation of the country's export-oriented business community in 1991. Those unseemly revelations came two years after German companies were caught aiding, abetting and profiting from Libyan nasty Muammar al-Qaddafi's chemical weapons program. As the world's pundits steamed over German "merchants of death," the government tightened export control laws, beefed up enforcement and stiffened penalties for violators. Decent, law-abiding businessmen bawled that they were being forced to pay for the sins of a few dirty rats. For their part, the rats secretly vowed that when there's a will to export death, there's a way.

For Snoopy, Maybe

RENT: EXORBITANT

*I*n late 1991, rent control in the eastern states was relaxed to allow the price for a square meter of apartment space to soar a possible 250%. Previously, rents had been kept extremely low, to under 5% of income, and landlords had been unable to undertake badly needed renovations. Still, in a country of rented-apartment dwellers, at a time of high unemployment and job insecurity, the pill was bitter. In urban areas in the West, a mismatch of supply and demand in the housing market continued to push up rents, already 20% to 30% of income, and small fortunes were often paid under the table for anything that became available. For "undesirables" (single women with children and dogs, for example) the struggle to find accommodation could become a nightmare.

1991 and 1992:
War in Europe, Asylum Tensions at Home

Yugoslavia Erupts in Civil War

BEACON OF HOPE
Refugees Head for Open German Door

Parties Tangle over Immigration Policy

Wave of Terror
RIGHTIST THUGS ATTACK REFUGEES

CANDLEPOWER
POPULAR PROTESTS
SLAM RIGHT-WING VIOLENCE

Vapid Deployment Force

When Yugoslavia, an artificial, multi-ethnic construct pasted together after World War II, exploded into civil war in 1991, the higher-horsepower European Community charged into the fray as mediator and peacemaker. At long last the Old Continent was finding its way to a common foreign-policy identity. Or not. In a barrage of proclamations,

communiqués, statements of intent and appeals for peace, Europe's leaders cried out for a halt to the bloodshed. But moral outrage doth not a policy make. The ghosts of wars past haunted Europe's Yugoslavia policy. Germany plumped for recognition of the breakaway republics of Croatia and Slovenia, two former Hapsburg lands. Britain and France hoped to keep Yugoslavia in one piece, tacitly supporting their former ally Serbia. As Europe horsed around, Yugoslavia burned.

Babes in Arms

While its allies bickered and carped, Germany took its boldest foreign-policy step since unification when it recognized Croatia and Slovenia as independent states in December 1991. Immediately those who blasted the Germans for sitting out the Persian Gulf war cursed them for muscling in on the Yugoslav one. It seemed that whatever it did or didn't, the new Germany was as damned as the old West Germany had been. The allies of that half-country had always wanted it to be strong enough to withstand the mighty Soviet Union, but not too strong to threaten tiny Luxembourg. So what flavor Germany did the world really want? The world didn't know, and frankly the Germans didn't either.

Chain of Command

*T*he Balkan war escalated in 1992 when Serbia assaulted Bosnia-Herzegovina and entangled five warring factions representing three ethnic groups in a savage guerrilla war in which the alliances were as blurry as the front lines. Serbian aerial bombardments and mortar fire reduced Sarajevo, site of the 1984 Winter Olympics, to a charred wasteland. As the world community looked on in horror, UN mediators vainly sought a peace arrangement. In a largely symbolic act, Germany sent the destroyer Bavaria into the Adriatic Sea to monitor the commercial blockade against Serbia. But it was a one-foot-in, one-foot-out operation. Since the German constitution forbade military action outside the NATO defense perimeter, the Bavaria's guns were spiked.

Westward Ho

The collapse of the old order in the hammer-and-sickle sphere brought a certain freedom from communist-style repression, but little freedom to live the good life which many thought would surely follow. Instead, as many countries descended into anarchy and repression, as long-suppressed ethnic resentments flared and led to civil war, as the state of the various national economies reached an unimaginable low, hundreds of thousands of desperate people fled westward for their lives. A large number of them made it to Germany. The more fortunate who could claim German ancestry could also claim German citizenship under German law. The rest could apply for political asylum. Fearful of mass migration from the East, the Germans pondered how to keep the East where it was.

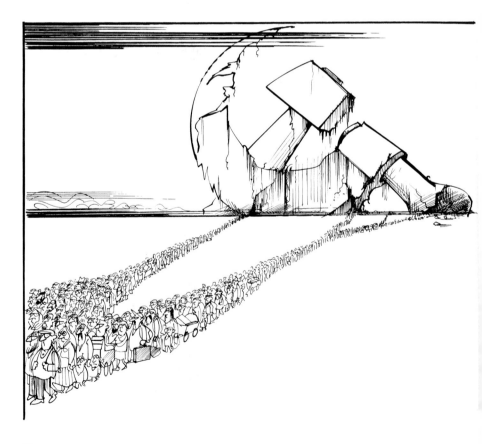

Safe-Haven Germany

With a unique provision of its constitution guaranteeing the individual right of political asylum, the Federal Republic was a logical haven for the politically persecuted of the world – and for many persecuted by other evils, not strictly political. But when the number of asylum seekers shot up dizzily after 1989, the open-arms policy came under heavy attack. Beset by their own problems, a growing number of German residents, native and otherwise, began demanding that something be done to halt the refugee "invasion" and "asylum abuse." The government was willing to accommodate, but needed support from the opposition Social Democrats to change the constitution. Consensus proved elusive.

Flight by Flight

      After much heated debate, a compromise was reached by the end of 1992. Only those who arrived in Germany without passing through another "safe" country – ideally, all of Germany's neighbors – would be eligible to apply for asylum. The rest would have to descend from heaven with a visa in hand or retrace their steps to the first safe country they had made it to on their odyssey. Refugees fleeing from war zones would be granted limited residence permits. With a solution to the constitutional impasse in sight, politicians of all colors were relieved. But the refugee problem remained, to be labeled "European" and shunted, like the refugees themselves, to a different authority.

Ladybird, Ladybird...

Determined to find a scapegoat for the social problems confronting the new Germany, a small but growing number of disturbed malcontents from the western as well as eastern states settled on the most visible and most helpless social group they could find: the dispossessed refugees. By September 1991, isolated acts of violence against foreigners (refugees or longtime legal residents, the perpetrators were not too choosy) were turning into more organized nastiness, as bands of neo-Nazi hooligans went on the rampage, setting fire to refugee quarters and forcing the evacuation of asylum seekers from towns like Hoyerswerda. Seemingly paralyzed, the authorities both local and national looked on and hoped the problem would solve itself.

Flaming Lunacy

It didn't. During the following year, xenophobic incidents increased dramatically. In August 1992, the country and the world were horrified by the unchecked days of arson and viciousness in Rostock, and the torching of the former concentration camp in Sachsenhausen. With the media shouting "shades of Weimar," even the most complacent Germans started to feel the heat. When, in November, a Turkish woman and two children were killed in an arson attack in Moelln, the government was galvanized into action. In a belated crackdown against the loony right, culprits were energetically pursued, organizations of the radical right outlawed and Nazi emblems banished. With a no-more-nonsense policy in effect, by the end of the year the incidents had ceased to dominate the headlines.

The Flicker Reaction

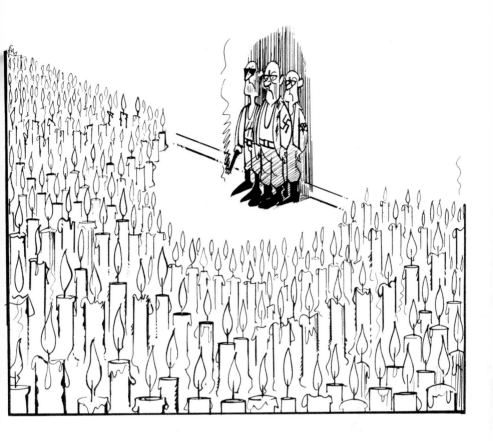

While the government wondered how to tackle the xenophobic disease, members of the public took the initiative to stem the epidemic. From Hoyerswerda on, groups of concerned citizens banded together to keep watch over refugee housing projects; others demonstrated in support of their foreign brethren. But it was the Moelln murders which mobilized the silent majority to turn out in the hundreds of thousands to express their disgust with the intolerance and violence of the radical right. With glowing candles and torches and lanterns, they marched through the cities and towns of Germany; almost half a million lights illuminated Munich at the beginning of December as one community after another took to the streets to show solidarity.

VOTERS SCORN GRIDLOCK, BLITZ TOP PARTIES

Strike Price
Work Stoppage Lames Economy

Time for Sainthood
GENSCHMAN RETIRES

World Biggies Meet in Munich

WIPEOUT!
EUROPE'S CURRENCIES GO BERSERK

SPD Blahs

*I*f the two years following unification were not too good
for Kohl and his coalition, they were no better for the directionless SPD.
True, they got young and handsome Björn Engholm to head the party and
play shadow chancellor, and young and handsome Hans-Ulrich Klose to
head the parliamentary group, but to little avail: the party stubbornly
refused to follow their leaders, who could not decide where to lead them
anyway. As they argued over how to stem the flood of refugees and how
to keep all Germans in uniform from taking part in foreign conflicts,
they threw away their chance to cash in on the unpopularity of the govern-
ing parties. The party's grand old men, Brandt and Schmidt, looked on
sadly and wondered (often aloud) what the new generation was coming to.

Bumpy Landings

Smoldering discontent with the direction Germany was headed in brought the two main parties down to earth with an unceremonious kaplonk in state elections in Schleswig-Holstein and Baden-Württemberg in April 1992. Like in other malaise-stricken western countries, angry citizens sent the ruling party a message that they were fed up with do-nothing politics and gridlock. Germans, however, differed from politics-weary voters elsewhere by sending a carbon copy of that message to the leading opposition party. Not only couldn't the SPD cash in on the CDU's woes, it took a nasty spill of its own. The only winners were right-wing parties playing on popular fears of crime, immigration and social unrest. The people wanted the incumbent bums thrown out, alright. But did they really want the right-wing bums put in?

Ham-Handed Tactics

With the eastern economy in a catatonic state and the western economy lurching into recession, life got very costly for a government that once prided itself on fiscal rectitude. Its chief cost-cutters – Finance Minister Theo Waigel and Defense Minister Volker Rühe – sprung into action in a made-for-the-evening-news sitcom entitled "Piggy Bank Power vs. the Porkmasters." To raise cash, Waigel came up with innovative measures that looked like taxes, smelled like taxes, tasted like taxes but were actually revenue enhancements. Rühe tried to persuade the military establishment it could defend the country without the pricey Jäger 90 fighter aircraft. After all, Austria was unlikely to attack.

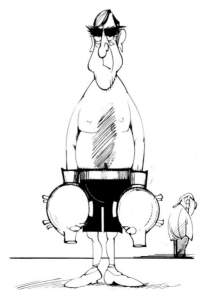

Wage Warfare

While the cost-cutters sharpened their knives, labor representatives wanted a belated cut of the profits of the post-Wall boom and went into the 1992 wage talks with lofty demands. The gulf between labor and management was so unbridgeable that the public-sector unions declared their first strike in twenty years. The trains didn't run, on time or otherwise. Undelivered mail piled high in unstaffed post offices. Airports were lamed by wildcat walkouts. Schools, daycare centers, even hospitals felt the pinch. And most bothering of all to those with sensitive sniffers, mountains of garbage lined the normally pristine streets. When all the negotiating was over and the strike was done, the unions settled for a 5.4% pay hike – the same raise they had rejected before starting the stoppage. Predictably, both the unions and government claimed victory.

Goodbye, Genschman

*T*he day the strike struck, Hans-Dietrich Genscher stole the unions' headlines by declaring he'd had a swell eighteen years as foreign minister but would prefer to leave both his and the world's problems to someone else. Namely to Helmut Kohl. But stepping down was not Genscher's style. The doyen of world diplomats could only step up. For the time being, Genscher sunned himself in Germany's favor from atop his lofty pedestal. How long he would stay above the fray was anyone's guess. Ever the country's most popular pol, Genschman was widely tipped as the best man for the German presidency (a largely ceremonial post) when that job becomes available in 1994.

Kinkel Takes the Reins

With the departure of Genschman, the Free Democrats were thrown into a tizzy. Determined to hang on to the top Foreign Ministry position, they dug into their ranks for a candidate of suitable stature, and failing to find an obvious one, came up with two. The party leadership choice, Housing Minister Irmgard Schwaetzer, was shot down by the grass roots, who managed to hoist Justice Minister Klaus Kinkel into the empty saddle. As the former secret service boss rode bravely into the international arena, he vowed to stick to the policy tracks of his illustrious predecessor and to negotiate the hurdles to German military participation in UN peacekeeping missions.

Lonely at the Top

MUNICH, JULY 1992 – The leaders of the world's top seven economies gather for some power breakfasting, lunching and supping in their first meeting in the united Germany. Helping Boris Yeltsin's crisis-ridden Russia and unblocking the GATT trade talks dominate the agenda. After two days of debating the world's unsolvable problems, the summitteers go home to their own unsolvable problems. Some go home for good. America's Bush is whacked out of office four months later, Canada's Mulroney calls it quits in early 1993. Nor are Britain's Major or France's Mitterand riding tidal waves of voter support. Even the once-invincible unity chancellor is plumbing the depths in the popularity ratings.

Balancing Act

*O*n August 22, 1992, coincidentally the day that the radical right went berserk in Rostock, the SPD announced a radical change of non-course. After a two-day top-level party pow wow, the Engholm faction decided to support an amendment to the constitution to tighten asylum laws and another to allow German troops to take part in UN peace-keeping missions outside NATO territory. Other party leaders, claiming to represent the grass roots, were outraged, but the Engholm initiative prevailed, albeit in slightly modified form, and at a special party session in November, a majority of the delegates paved the way for a December compromise with the coalition. But the constitutional kerfuffle lasted well into 1993.

Monetary Malcontents

When we last checked, Europe was marching slowly but purposefully toward a single currency sometime before the year 2000. Then, in September 1992, our unsuspecting mate Michel looked skyward and saw it was raining cats, dogs and other people's money. Devalued currencies splattered on the pavement below. What caused the cloudburst? Europe's currency stabilization mechanism had "imploded," explained the monetary meteorologists. In the same breath, many accused Germany's Bundesbank of seeding the European clouds with high interest rates meant to choke off domestic inflation. Bundesbankers brushed aside these charges. The real rainmakers, they said, were politicians elsewhere in Europe who tried to inflate and deficit-spend their way to economic prosperity.

HONI REDUX

Honi Soit Qui Mal Y Pense
(He Who Thinks Evil of It Should
Be in Honi's Shoes)

*In Which We Trace the Continuing Saga of the Grand
and Garbled Ex-Kingpin of the Irrepressible German
Democratic Republic*

GOTCHA!
Honi Thrown into the Klink

BOTCHA!
Honi Slips Out in Moscow Escape Ploy

No Place Like Home
HONI BOOTED BACK FOR BERLIN TRIAL

FREE AT LAST!
Court Releases Ailing Honi

Chilling Out
Honi Hangs Loose in Balmy Chile

Nailing Honi Down

When we last saw Honi (see page 21), he was Humpty Dumpty in front of his wall. In his case though, the King's men were more interested in legally nailing him than in putting him together again, a task which was to prove just as impossible. While Honi was morally guilty of everything from murder to the economic destruction of a country and the repression of its people, his legal guilt was not too clear. Were his misdeeds ordinary punishable crimes or "acts of state"? Had Honi acted within his rights as leader of a sovereign country, or was he guilty of crimes against humanity? The legal beavers prepared to go to battle, and a warrant for Honi's arrest was issued in December 1989.

Moscow Olé!

Honi's prison life was short. Supposedly dying of cancer, the eighty-year-old was removed to a Potsdam military hospital under Russian protection in April 1990, and in March 1991, transferred "secretly" to Moscow. The Germans formally demanded him back, but Gorbi thumbed his nose (giving rise to rumors of collusion). By September, with Gorbi powerless and Yeltsin threatening to extradite his troublesome guest, Honi felt it prudent to beat a hasty retreat to the Chilean embassy, where he holed up for 232 days. The Germans dutifully protested, but with Honi on the hop, he was one headache less. But headaches return, and so did Honi. On July 29, 1992, he flew into Berlin and into the arms of the representatives of German justice.

Due Process of Law

*T*he trial against Honi and the Honettes (including Mielke the Stasi and four other GDR heavies) began in November 1992. From the beginning a tour de farce, it never got off the ground. Since the mental and physical health of the accused had to be taken into account, the elderly gents had little trouble rearranging and postponing the proceedings. Honi, as sprightly and defiant as ever, had only to announce he wasn't feeling well for the wheels of justice to grind to a halt. And so it might have continued for years, if the Berlin court had not abruptly and arbitrarily decided to end the whole embarrassment. On January 14, it allowed Honi to leave the country, destination Chile, where he was given a hero's welcome. Today, Honi is alive, unrepentant and remarkably well (say the doctors at the hospital in Santiago where Honi is an outpatient). Honi soit...

The Little Fish

With Honi off the hook, and no justice in sight for his fellow sharks, what should happen to the countless smaller fish in the murky waters of GDR crime and corruption? At the beginning of January 1992, the first verdicts in the trials of former border guards were handed down. Accused of killing a young man trying to dash to freedom, two guards were given prison sentences. Yet, it was Honi and his henchmen who were the architects of the deadly "anti-fascist protective wall" the length of the border and around Berlin, and who ordered the guards to shoot. And, if necessary, to kill. In all, two hundred died. With Honi now basking in the sun, fair trials for his agents can only end in like punishment – free one-way tickets to Chile.

Economy Crunched by Unity Costs

JOBBERWACKY!
Unemployment Heading Up

Sick Fix
Health Reform Puts Clamp on Costs

COALITION CREAKS
AND GROANS

BELLY FLOP
Kohl Dives in Popularity Polls

Don't Look Down

"This is the hour of truth," announced Kohl lugubriously to his fellow Christian Democrats at a party meeting in October 1992. Given the rather awful state of economic affairs, great sacrifice was called for to seal the gaping hole in the country's finances and keep the nation – particularly the eastern part of it – afloat. Germany's five leading economic institutes confirmed that they had been a tad optimistic in their economic forecasts, which they downgraded for the second time since January. It could be, they said, that the economy of united Germany might further shrink in the first quarter of 1993 as Germany entered what they called a "mini recession."

The Budgetary Arts

    Eagerly anticipated by critics all across Germany, the 1993 federal budget proved even more artful than its predecessors. Was the finance minister doing his impression of an elongated donut standing on tiptoe? Art appreciators differed over how to interpret his bold stroke of creative genius. Not only did the government sculpt a federal budget, but also a supporting group of shadow budgets, sub-budgets, secondary budgets, ancillary budgets, discretionary budgets, off-budgets and off-off budgets. When put together in a time-and-motion study, the collected budgets and non-budgets added up to a general government deficit of over DM 200 billion for 1993. Let no one claim the government is cutting spending on the arts.

Time Bomb

*T*here are small lies, big lies and statistics. The truth
about unemployment in the eastern states can be fiddled every which
way, depending on how bad the news is supposed to sound. Official
figures put unemployment in the East in the fall of 1992 at around 13.5%,
with just over a million jobless. But another two million easterners are
involved in job creation, job retention, job training and job retraining
programs established by the government to soften the unemployment
blow, and these confuse the issue and the figures. A fact is that two of
every five eastern German workers have lost their jobs since 1989.
With predictions that the total eastern workforce will dwindle yet further
to under six million in 1993, the situation is explosive.

The Holey Net

Oh! for the good old days of bounteous social benefits and true social security, when the contributors felt no pain and the recipients didn't know how good they had it. Those days have not quite gone forever, but the social safety net is showing holes. With unemployment up and contributions down, with a population of too many old and too few young, with all the extra burdens of unification, recession and migration, there just ain't enough money to share among the needy. Cut down the benefits, say some; raise contributions, say others; put the burden on the taxpayer, put it on the private sector. Let the people take care of themselves, shout the free marketeers. Economize, screams the government, to whom it no longer knows.

Gesundheit

Deputized by the chancellor to get a handle on the slippery health-care system, Health Minister Horst Seehofer wrestled with a multi-tentacled beast. In 1992 public health insurers gasped their way to record deficits. Pill makers, pill prescribers and pill poppers – that is, pharmaceuticals companies, doctors and patients – agreed that costs were running out of control. In an attempt to bandage the system, the minister came up with a cunning plan to cause the greatest suffering for the greatest number: drug makers would charge less, patients pay more and doctors earn less. Although opponents predicted it would mean the end of Western civilization as we know it, the reform package made it into law. And the public uproar continues – proof positive of the plan's brilliance.

Kohl's Woes

"**W**hat's one annus horribilis?" asked King Kohl of Queen Liz at the end of 1992. "I've already had two, with no relief in sight." With his great achievement, German unity, giving him a royal migraine as all the problems descended on his head, and with everybody griping from goony left to loony right – well, what on earth was he supposed to do with economic crisis, social unrest, hoards of refugees and match-happy hooligans? Good grief, he couldn't even count on his own top people; his stamp-and-phone minister left in a huff over his non-policy in ex-Yugoslavia, his take-care-of-business minister left in disgrace after signing improper autographs, and a couple of the rest were just waiting for him to fall. And then in March, the Hessians refused to cheer him on (see page 114). It makes a man wonder.

THE GREAT
UNITY CHANCELLOR
H. KOHL

DEC.2,1990

Hillibilly and Helmut

Some guys have all the luck. Hillary's husband, pictured upper left, won the White House in November 1992 on the promise of a middle-class tax "cut." Once in office, he discovered to his horror that he had mispronounced one of the words in his campaign stump speech. Instead of a "cut," he should have been promising a "hike." Immediately he issued a correction, muddling the American middle classes. And yet they saluted him as the second coming of George Washington. When the unity chancellor attempted a similar sleight-of-tongue, he was briskly condemned and nearly booed off the political stage. Are the Germans less grateful than the Americans? Or just less gullible?

SOLIDARITY!
Parties Pass Panacea Pact

Sibling Quibbling
The German-German Love Affair

Big Parties Pooped in Local Elections

SPD HEADLESS
Party Desperately Seeking Savior

Bonn Booms, Berlin Waits

Pacting It In

As the mountain of public debt rose beyond DM 1.2 trillion, a panicky government aired possible ways to pay the unification bill: obligatory and/or voluntary interest-free loans to the public purse, another temporary solidarity tax, a super tax for better earners, drastic cuts in public spending, wage freezes – or any combination thereof. While the SPD talked of "sheer financial chaos" and the taxpaying population fretted, a new Kohlian buzzword made the rounds: Solidarity Pact. After months of haggling and floating of trial balloons, federal and state government bigwigs holed up in March 1993 to put the finishing touches on a compromise to dump more money into the lumbering economy. To pay for the program, all kinds of taxes would go up. But sneakily enough, not until after the December 1994 national elections.

Brotherly Love I: The Man Who Came to Dinner

At first, it was all sibling love. "We are one people" chanted the east-siders (Ossis) at their Monday evening get-togethers in Leipzig in those heady, pre-unity days, and their voices were echoed by the west-siders (Wessis) over the border. And so they became one people and the joy was (still) great. But not for long. The strong, successful Wessis poured into Ossi-land, now D-Markland, now their land, and found its people to be lacking – in energy, initiative, know-how, and all those other qualities that made a Wessi what he was. And worse: the Ossis were poor and riddled with debt, and expected the Wessis to give them a hand. "We'll show you how we do things in D-Markland," said the Wessis, as they installed themselves and took charge.

Brotherly Love II: It's All in the Mind

As it dawned on the Ossis that the Wessi Way was fraught with dangers such as soaring costs and unemployment, that the better life might be a long way off and that in the meantime, equality was just another word, they came to resent their bossy, arrogant saviors, who in turn shouted, "Ingrates! We're emptying our pockets to help you, there's no end in sight, and you want more, more, more." "We're the ones who paid in spades for the sins of our common fathers," replied the Ossis. "We want no charity, just our rights." And lo and behold, another wall began to split the people asunder, a wall in the mind.

Dino-might

Voters continued their hit-and-run attacks on incumbent politicians and dawdling parties by sending them a toothy message in the March 1993 local elections in the western state of Hesse. Not only did an uncommonly high 30% boycott the ballot altogether, those who did vote gave disturbingly strong support to right-wing anti-parties which promised in policy-less platforms to solve the unemployment and housing crises, crack down on asylum and welfare cheats, head off autobahn fees, end waste, corruption and nepotism and generally clean house. In short, to do everything the geriatric establishment was incapable of doing. Whether the promise-'em-anything right can parlay its 8.3% showing in Hesse into consistent political clout remains to be seen. But one thing has been seen already: the hapless major parties running scared.

Björn Never Again

Steaming right along, the Engholm-led SPD was all set (it hoped) to torpedo Captain Kohl in the 1994 national elections until Engholm himself was sunk by a murky scandal from political yesteryear. When pipe-puffing Björn went under in May 1993, party poobahs pondered how to steer the rudderless SPD back into fighting trim. Several of them, with name recognition and without, vied for the thankless honor of becoming the drifting party's fifth chancellor candidate in as many elections. They'll need stamina. Because when this definitive history went to press, the search for a certified Kohl-buster was only just beginning. In the SPD (and not only there), the saga of political disarray is very much To Be Continued.

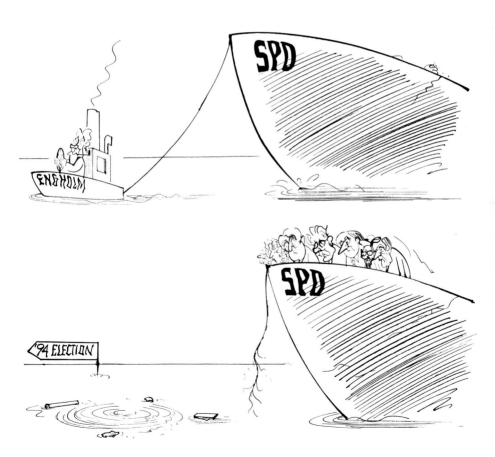

Bonbon for Bonn

Almost two years after the much-debated, fiercely fought and, in the end, narrow decision to move the government from provisional Bonn to capital Berlin within ten years (or so), the song goes on. With the country's finances looking recessed and unlikely to pick up for a while to come, with calls to save, save, save resounding in the nation's ears, it requires brilliant rhetoric to justify a move which will cost between DM 13.2 and DM 100 billion – a king's ransom by anybody's reckoning. So while some are suggesting that the move be put off for yet another decade, others are suggesting that it be put off altogether. Bonn remains serene, as it continues to build as if there were a tomorrow, while power-less Berlin may have to settle for the 2000 Olympics – if it's lucky. It's a bear to be Berlin these days.

Ich bin ein Berliner

But this bearish sentiment doesn't wash with Richard von Weizsäcker, Germany's president (and a former mayor of West Berlin), who in March 1993 decided to move his official residence to Berlin in a bid to end the dithering. Increasingly impatient with the political establishment, the eminently respected head of state, whose second and last term ends in mid-1994, has verbally entered the fray on a number of issues, from Ossi-Wessi harmony to Germany's global responsibilities. But calling in the movers was unusual unilateral action. Citizens of Berlin took heart. Eventually, they know, the government will be theirs. Until then, they'll grin and bear it.

In Lieu of an Epilogue

*H*appily immersed in history-as-it-happens, our trio of cartoon-sifting, pun-toting sleuths – Hanel, Stern and Neuger – was coming closer and closer to unlocking the German Riddle when, in early May 1993, they were struck by an awful realization: their conveniently forgotten deadline was looming.

Except for a good hanging, nothing concentrates the mind like a looming deadline. Only for our three, the timing couldn't have been worse. Events in Germany weren't cooperating. Instead of settling into post-unity predictability, they were hurtling every which way. History-as-it-happens just refused to stop happening. And our intrepid troika was swept up in it.

Every tip, however inconsequential it first seemed, opened up promising avenues of inquiry. Tracking one lead, our gumshoes watched as cabinet ministers and other political mighties were herded into the woodshed. One got axed for sticking the taxpayer with his moving and housecleaning bills, another for sticking the same with her interior decorating bill. Another pol was shooed from office for aggravated influence-peddling, and yet another was under pressure for consorting with shady characters.

Not all clues led to the ridiculous, however. Some led to the critical policy issues of the day. How would the government master the ballooning budget deficit, spreading recession, lengthening unemployment lines, lingering Ossi-Wessi tensions, mounting furor over German participation or nonparticipation in NATO and UN peacekeeping missions, thickening threats to western European integration, deepening worries over eastern European stability, etcetera, etcetera? Our detectives were loath to put their report to bed while the stakeout was still in progress.

But a deadline is a deadline. The knowledge that this wacky history must come to an end drove the trio into one last Sherlock Holmesian frenzy, in which loose ends were tied up, informants discreetly paid off, T's crossed, I's dotted, names left unchanged to torment the innocent and you-heard-it-here-first conclusions drawn.

Two conclusions, to be exact. One is that for all its bellyaching, breast-beating, hand-wringing and finger-pointing, Germany is indeed in the pink. In fact, it is as frisky, bouncy and playful as it has ever been. The second conclusion is that if the Germans were truly wise, they'd sit back and enjoy it. Not only is their country excruciatingly funny – it's getting funnier by the day.